Recipe Notes

All spoon measures are level:
1 tablespoon = 15ml spoon;
1 teaspoon = 5ml spoon.

Follow EITHER metric or Imperial measures and NEVER mix in one recipe as they are not interchangeable.

If preferred, use margarine for pastry instead of butter; white vegetable fat instead of lard.

Eggs used are a medium size 3 unless otherwise stated.

For additional hints and tips on pastry making, see step-by-step instructions and pictures on pages 18-19 and 34-35.

Kilojoules and kilocalories at the end of each recipe are represented by the letters kJ and kcal.

This edition published 1994 by Merehurst Limited
Ferry House, 51-57 Lacy Road, Putney, London SW15 1PR

Copyright © Gräfe und Unzer GmbH 1993, Munich

ISBN 1 874567 21 2

All rights reserved

Designed by Clive Dorman & Co.

Printed in Italy by G. Canale & C.S.p.A

Distributed in the UK by J.B. Fairfax Press Limited,
9 Trinity Centre, Park Farm, Wellingborough, Northants NN8 6ZB

Distributed in Australia by J.B. Fairfax Press Pty Ltd,
80 McLachlan Avenue, Rushcutters Bay, Sydney, NSW 2011

Courgette Quiche

Serves 6

A tasty vegetable quiche, generously spiked with garlic.

Preparation time: about 1 hour
Baking time: 25-30 minutes

FOR BAKING
25cm/10in greased fluted flan tin or dish

SHORTCRUST PASTRY
250g (8oz/2 cups) plain flour
Pinch of salt
125g (4oz) cold butter or mixture of butter
   and lard
90ml (3fl oz/⅓ cup) cold water to mix

FILLING
625g (1¼ lb) small courgettes (zucchini)
4 cloves garlic
3 tablespoons sunflower or corn oil
Salt to taste
4 eggs
100g (3½ oz) Cheddar cheese, grated
2 tablespoons snipped fresh chives
30g (1oz) plain flour
280ml (9fl oz/1 cup) milk

1 To make pastry, sift flour and salt into bowl. Using round-bladed knife, cut in butter until mixture resembles breadcrumbs. Gradually add water and mix to fairly stiff but pliable dough. Knead dough quickly until smooth and shape into ball. Put on to plate, cover with plastic wrap and chill for 1 hour. Roll out pastry fairly thinly into round on lightly floured work surface. Use to line tin or dish. Trim top edges with sharp knife. Chill pastry case for 15 minutes.

2 Preheat oven to 230C/450F/Gas 8.

3 Top and tail courgettes (zucchini). Cut into 3cm (1¼ in) thick slices.

4 Peel garlic and cut into thin slivers. Heat oil in frying pan. Add garlic and sauté over moderate heat until pale golden. Stir in courgettes (zucchini). Continue to cook briskly for about 5 minutes, stirring. Season with salt. Cool.

5 Gently prick pastry base with fork. Separate 1 egg. Brush a little egg white over fork holes. Cover with courgette (zucchini) and garlic mixture, then sprinkle with cheese and chives.

6 In small bowl or jug, mix flour with a little of the milk until smooth. Stir in remaining milk. Beat in remaining egg white, yolk and whole eggs. Season with salt. Pour into quiche over filling.

7 Bake quiche for 25-30 minutes until just set and golden brown. If necessary, cover pastry with foil towards end of cooking to prevent overbrowning. Turn out quiche on to plate or serve from tin or dish.

Nutritional value per portion:
about 3100kJ/740kcal
Protein: 25g
Fat: 48g
Carbohydrate: 49g

Courgette Quiche

Ham Quiche

Serves 6

A versatile quiche perfect for a light lunch or supper dish.

Preparation time: about 1 hour
Baking time: 20-25 minutes

FOR BAKING
6 small 10cm/4in greased fluted flan tins

SHORTCRUST PASTRY
250g (8oz/2 cups) plain flour
Pinch of salt
125g (4oz) cold butter or mixture of butter
 and lard
90ml (3fl oz/⅓ cup) cold water to mix

FILLING
220g (7oz) lean ham
90g (3oz) Gouda or Cheddar cheese,
 grated
2 eggs
155ml (5fl oz/⅔ cup) whipping cream
2 tablespoons snipped fresh chives
Salt to taste
Snipped fresh chives for garnishing

1 To make pastry, sift flour and salt into bowl. Using round-bladed knife, cut in butter until mixture resembles breadcrumbs. Gradually add water and mix to fairly stiff but pliable dough. Knead dough quickly until smooth and shape into ball. Put on to plate, cover with plastic wrap and chill for 1 hour. Divide pastry into 6 equal pieces. Roll each piece thinly to a round on lightly floured work surface. Use to line tins. Trim away surplus pastry from top edges with sharp knife. Chill for 15 minutes.

2 Coarsely chop ham.

3 Preheat oven to 230C/450F/Gas 8.

4 Gently prick pastry bases with fork. Fill with ham and cheese.

5 Whisk eggs and cream together in jug. Stir in chives. Season lightly with salt. Pour egg mixture over filling.

6 Bake quiches for 25-30 minutes until just set and golden brown. If necessary, cover pastry with foil towards end of cooking to prevent overbrowning. Turn out quiches on to plates or serve from tin or dish. Garnish with snipped fresh chives.

Nutritional value per portion:
about 3200kJ/760kcal
Protein: 26g
Fat: 55g
Carbohydrate: 39g

Ham Quiche

Leek Quiche

Serves 6

A succulent and deliciously-flavoured quiche, perfect for vegetarians.

Preparation time: about 1 hour
Baking time: 30 minutes

FOR BAKING
25cm/10in greased fluted flan tin or dish

SHORTCRUST PASTRY
250g (8oz/2 cups) plain flour
Pinch of salt
125g (4oz) cold butter or mixture of butter and white vegetable fat
90ml (3 fl oz/⅓ cup) cold water to mix

FILLING
2 medium leeks
1 medium carrot
15g (½ oz) butter or margarine
45g (1½ oz) sunflower seeds
3 tablespoons water
3 eggs
2 tablespoons plain flour
155ml (5fl oz/⅔ cup) milk
250ml (8fl oz/1 cup) thick soured cream
Salt to taste
Freshly milled pepper
90g (3oz) Emmental or Edam cheese, grated

1 To make pastry, sift flour and salt into bowl. Using round-bladed knife, cut in butter until mixture resembles breadcrumbs. Gradually add water and mix to fairly stiff but pliable dough. Knead dough until smooth and shape into ball. Cover with plastic wrap and chill for 1 hour. Roll out pastry thinly into round on lightly floured work surface. Use to line tin or dish. Trim top edges with sharp knife. Chill for 15 minutes.

2 Trim leeks and slice thinly. Cut carrot into very thin slices.

3 Melt butter or margarine in saucepan. Add sunflower seeds. Sauté for about 1 minute, stirring. Add carrot slices and water. Cover with lid and simmer gently for 7 minutes, stirring occasionally. Add leeks. Cover pan and continue to simmer for a further 5 minutes. Cool.

4 Preheat oven to 230C/450F/Gas 8.

5 Gently prick pastry base with fork. Separate 1 egg. Brush a little egg white over fork holes. Fill with leek mixture.

6 In small bowl or jug, mix flour with a little of the milk until smooth then stir in remaining milk. Beat in egg white, yolk, whole eggs, soured cream, salt and pepper.

7 Sprinkle vegetables with cheese. Spoon over the egg and milk mixture.

8 Bake quiche for 30 minutes until just set and golden brown. If necessary, cover pastry with foil towards end of cooking to prevent overbrowning. Turn out quiche on to plate or serve from tin or dish.

Nutritional value per portion:
about 2900kJ/690
Protein: 20g
Fat: 46g
Carbohydrate: 40g

Leek Quiche

Minced Beef Quiche

Serves 6

A substantial quiche with a strong beefy flavour.

Preparation time: about 50 minutes
Baking time: 30-40 minutes

FOR BAKING
25cm/10in greased fluted flan tin or dish

SHORTCRUST PASTRY
280g (9oz/2 cups) plain flour
Pinch of salt
140g (4½ oz) cold butter or mixture of butter
and lard
100ml (3½ fl oz/⅓ cup) cold water to mix

FILLING
½ green, ½ red pepper (capsicum)
1 small onion
1 tablespoon sunflower or corn oil
375g (12oz) lean minced beef
100g (3½ oz) low-fat soft cheese or fromage
frais
½ teaspoon dry mustard
Salt to taste
Pinch of dried marjoram
2 eggs
30g (1oz) rolled porridge oats
1 egg white

1 To make pastry, sift flour and salt into
bowl. Using round-bladed knife, cut in
butter until mixture resembles breadcrumbs.
Add water and mix to stiff dough. Knead
until smooth. Cover and chill for 1 hour.

2 Reserve 125g (4oz) pastry. Roll remain-
der into round on floured work surface.
Use to line tin or dish. Trim edges with sharp
knife. Chill pastry case with reserved pastry

for 15 minutes. Roll out reserved pastry on
lightly floured work surface. Cut into 2.5cm
(1in) wide strips, see pages 18-19.

3 Preheat oven to 230C/450F/Gas 8.

4 De-seed pepper (capsicum) halves and
chop flesh finely. Peel and chop onion.

5 Heat 2 tsp oil in frying pan. Add onions
and sauté gently until transparent and
just beginning to soften. Add peppers and
minced beef. Stir-fry fairly briskly until meat
becomes dryish and crumbly.

6 Put soft cheese or fromage frais into
bowl with mustard, salt, marjoram, eggs
and oats and mix well. Combine with meat
mixture. Gently prick pastry base with fork.
Brush fork holes with a little egg white. Cover
with meat mixture and spread level.

7 Arrange strips in criss-cross pattern over
filling. Brush with remaining oil.

8 Bake quiche for 25-30 minutes until just
set and golden. If necessary, cover
pastry with foil towards end of cooking to
prevent overbrowning. Turn out or serve
from tin or dish.

Nutritional value per portion:
3100kJ/740kcal
Protein: 38g
Fat: 39g
Carbohydrate: 60g

Minced Beef Quiche

Asparagus Quiches

Serves 6

A pretty-coloured quiche, designed for late spring when asparagus starts making its annual appearance. It is on the costly side to make, but well worth every penny.

Preparation time: about 1 hour
Baking time: 20-25 minutes

FOR BAKING
6 small 10cm (4in) greased fluted flan tins

SHORTCRUST PASTRY
250g (8oz/2cups) plain flour
Pinch of salt
125g (4oz) cold butter or mixture of butter
    and lard
90ml (3fl oz/$\frac{1}{3}$ cup) cold water to mix

FILLING
750g (1$\frac{1}{2}$ lb) asparagus spears
Salt to taste
$\frac{1}{2}$ teaspoon caster sugar
3 eggs
155ml (5 fl oz/$\frac{2}{3}$ cup) single (light) cream
Pinch of cayenne pepper
60g (2oz) Edam or Cheddar cheese, grated

1 To make pastry, sift flour and salt into bowl. Using round-bladed knife, cut in butter until mixture resembles breadcrumbs. Gradually add water and mix to fairly stiff but pliable dough. Knead dough until smooth and shape into ball. Put on to plate, cover with plastic wrap and chill for 1 hour. Divide pastry into 6 equal pieces. Roll each piece thinly into rounds on lightly floured work surface. Use to line tins. Trim edges with sharp knife. Chill for 15 minutes.

2 Peel asparagus spears. Cut tough ends off each spear, two-thirds of the way down from tips. Cut spears into 5cm/2in

lengths. Simmer asparagus gently in boiling water, with salt and sugar, for 7 minutes, keeping pan partially covered.

3 Gently prick pastry bases with fork. Separate 1 egg. Brush a little egg white over fork holes.

4 Preheat oven to 230C/450F/Gas 8.

5 Tip remaining egg white, yolk and whole eggs into jug. Whisk in cream and cayenne pepper and season with salt.

6 Drain asparagus thoroughly and cool completely. Arrange over quiche bases. Sprinkle with cheese, then spoon egg and cream mixture over filling.

7 Bake quiches for 20-25 minutes until just set and golden brown. If necessary, cover pastry with foil towards end of cooking to prevent overbrowning. Turn out on to plates or serve from tins or dishes.

Nutritional value per portion:
2600kJ/620kcal
Protein: 19g
Fat: 42g
Carbohydrate: 42g

Asparagus Quiches

Farmer's Onion Quiche

Serves 6

This quiche is rich and robustly-flavoured, ideal with a glass of lightly-chilled crisp white wine or brown ale.

Preparation time: about 1 hour
Baking time: 30-35 minutes

FOR BAKING
25cm/10in greased fluted flan tin or dish.

SHORTCRUST PASTRY
250g (8oz/2cups) plain flour
Pinch of salt
125g (4oz) cold butter or mixture of butter
and lard
90ml (3fl oz/⅓ cup) cold water to mix

FILLING
625g (1¼ lb) onions
3 tablespoons sunflower or corn oil
100g (3½ oz) streaky bacon rashers, rinds
removed
2 eggs
60g (2oz) Edam or Emmental cheese,
grated
1 tablespoon plain flour
250ml (8fl oz/1 cup) milk
Salt to taste
Freshly milled pepper
Chopped fresh parsley for garnishing

1 To make pastry, sift flour and salt into bowl. Using round-bladed knife, cut in butter until mixture resembles breadcrumbs. Gradually add water and mix to fairly stiff but pliable dough. Knead dough until smooth and shape into ball. Put on to plate, cover with plastic wrap and chill for 1 hour. Roll pastry thinly into round on lightly floured work surface. Use to line tin or dish. Trim top edges with sharp knife. Chill for 15 minutes.

2 Peel onions and halve each one with sharp knife. Cut halves into thin slices. Sauté onions gently in oil in large frying pan until transparent and beginning to soften. Remove from pan; drain on kitchen paper.

3 Chop bacon coarsely. Add to pan in which onions were cooked and sauté until lightly browned. Remove from pan and drain on kitchen paper.

4 Preheat oven to 230C/450F/Gas 8.

5 Gently prick pastry base with fork. Separate 1 egg. Brush a little egg white over fork holes. Fill quiche with onions and bacon. Sprinkle with cheese.

6 In small bowl or jug, mix flour with a little of the milk until smooth. Stir in remaining milk. Beat in remaining egg white, yolk and whole egg. Season with salt and pepper and spoon into quiche.

7 Bake quiche for 30-35 minutes until just set and golden brown. If necessary, cover pastry with foil towards end of cooking to prevent overbrowning. Turn out quiche on to plate. Sprinkle top with chopped parsley.

Nutritional value per portion:
2700kJ/640kcal
Protein: 20g
Fat: 35g
Carbohydrate: 62g

14

Farmer's Onion Quiche

Tomato Quiche

Serves 6

A fresh-flavoured, light quiche, especially delicious made with summer-ripe tomatoes.

Preparation time: about 1 hour
Baking time: about 25-30 minutes

FOR BAKING
25cm/10in greased fluted flan tin or dish

SHORTCRUST PASTRY
280g (9oz/2 cups) plain flour
Pinch of salt
140g (4½ oz) cold butter or mixture of butter
   and lard
100ml (3½ fl oz/⅓ cup) cold water to mix

FILLING
1 small onion
625g (1¼ lb) ripe tomatoes
375g (12oz) Mozzarella cheese
·12 fresh basil leaves
2 eggs
100g (3½ oz) crème fraîche
1 teaspoon paprika
salt to taste
1 teaspoon sunflower or corn oil

1 To make pastry, sift flour and salt into bowl. Using round-bladed knife, cut in butter until mixture resembles breadcrumbs. Add water and mix to fairly stiff dough. Knead until smooth and shape into ball. Cover with plastic wrap and chill for 1 hour. Reserve 125g (4oz) pastry and chill. ·

2 Roll out remaining pastry fairly thinly into round on lightly floured work surface. Use to line prepared tin or dish. Trim away surplus pastry from top edges with sharp knife. Chill pastry case for 15 minutes.

3 Roll out reserved pastry fairly thinly. Cut into 2cm (¾ in) wide strips, see pages 18-19. Transfer strips to plate, cover with plastic wrap and chill until needed.

4 Preheat oven to 230C/450F/Gas 8.

5 Peel and finely chop onion. Cover tomatoes with boiling water for 30 seconds, plunge into cold water and peel away skins. Cut tomatoes into medium-thick slices. Slice cheese fairly thinly. Cut basil into fine shreds.

6 Gently prick pastry base with fork. Separate 1 egg. Brush a little egg white over fork holes. Fill quiche with tomatoes and cheese. Sprinkle with onion.

7 Beat remaining egg white in jug with yolk and whole egg. Whisk in crème fraîche and paprika. Stir in basil and season with salt. Spoon into quiche.

8 Arrange pastry strips in criss-cross pattern over top of quiche, brushing pastry with oil. Bake quiche for 25-30 minutes until just set and golden brown. If necessary, cover pastry with foil towards end of cooking to prevent overbrowning. Turn out quiche on to plate or serve from tin or dish.

Nutritional value per portion:
3500kJ/830kcal
Protein: 28g
Fat: 55g
Carbohydrate: 53g

Tomato Quiche

Step-by step

EGG, FLOUR AND MILK MIXTURE

1 Mix flour with a little of the measured liquid to make a smooth paste.

2 Add remaining milk, eggs and/or cream. Whisk until smooth.

3 Season mixture as recommended in recipe, but take care not to over-salt as some of the filling ingredients, such as bacon and cheese, can be quite salty.

QUICHE LID

4 Roll out quiche lid from reserved pastry. Transfer to board or plate and cover well with plastic wrap.Chill until needed.

5 Place pastry on top of filled quiche. Pinch edges of lid and pastry case together firmly to seal.

6 Using pointed kitchen knife, make small hole in centre of pastry to allow steam to escape and prevent pastry becoming soggy. Decorate with fancy pastry shapes, cut from trimmings, and dampened with water to hold them in place. Brush top with oil or beaten egg.

PASTRY STRIPS

7 Roll out reserved pastry fairly thinly on lightly floured work surface. Cut into strips of required width, with pastry wheel or knife using plastic ruler as guide.

8 Carefully transfer pastry strips to board or plate. Cover well with plastic wrap and chill for about 15 minutes.

9 Arrange pastry strips in criss-cross pattern over quiche. Brush each pastry strip with oil or beaten egg.

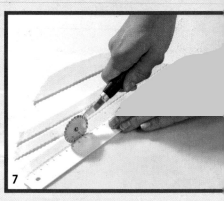

3

6

9

Quiche Lorraine

Serves 6

A traditional favourite with a succulent filling of bacon and eggs.

Preparation time: 1 hour
Baking time: 30 minutes

FOR BAKING
25cm/10in greased fluted flan tin or dish

SHORTCRUST PASTRY
250g (8oz/2cups) plain flour
Pinch of salt
125g (4oz) cold butter or mixture of butter
  and lard
90ml (3fl oz/⅓ cup) cold water to mix

FILLING
2 shallots
60g (2oz) streaky bacon rashers, rinds
  removed
15g (½ oz) margarine
2 tablespoons plain flour
375ml (12fl oz/1½ cups) milk
3 eggs
Salt to taste
1 teaspoon paprika
60g (2oz) Gruyère cheese, grated
Chopped fresh parsley for garnishing

1 To make pastry, sift flour and salt into bowl. Using round-bladed knife, cut in butter until mixture resembles breadcrumbs. Gradually add water and mix to fairly stiff but pliable dough. Knead dough quickly until smooth and shape into ball. Put on to plate, cover with plastic wrap and chill for 1 hour. Roll out pastry fairly thinly into round on lightly floured work surface. Use to line tin or dish. Trim top edges with sharp knife. Chill for 15 minutes.

2 Peel shallots and finely chop. Chop bacon. Melt margarine in frying pan and sauté shallots and bacon until pale golden.

3 Preheat oven to 230C/450F/Gas 8.

4 In small bowl or jug, mix flour with a little milk until smooth. Stir in remaining milk. Beat in remaining egg white, yolk, whole eggs, salt and paprika.

5 Gently prick pastry base with fork. Fill quiche with shallots, bacon and cheese. Carefully spoon in egg and milk mixture.

6 Bake quiche for about 30 minutes until just set and golden brown. If necessary, cover pastry with foil towards end of cooking to prevent overbrowning. Turn out quiche on to plate or serve from tin or dish. Sprinkle top with parsley.

Nutritional value per portion:
2900kJ/690kcal
Protein: 19g
Fat: 46g
Carbohydrate: 50g

Quiche Lorraine

Sweetcorn Quiche

Serves 6

An American-style filling of chicken and sweetcorn makes an original and satisfying quiche.

Preparation time: about 1 hour
Baking time: about 30 minutes

FOR BAKING
25cm/10in greased fluted flan tin or dish

SHORTCRUST PASTRY
250g (8oz/2 cups) plain flour
Pinch of salt
125g (4oz) cold butter or mixture of butter
and lard
90ml (3fl oz/⅓ cup) cold water to mix

FILLING
185g (6oz) cold cooked chicken
2 eggs
1 small courgette (zucchini)
2 spring onions (green shallots)
250g (8oz) sweetcorn, thawed and well
drained if frozen
100g (3½ oz) mascarpone cheese
Salt to taste
Freshly milled pepper
60g (2oz) Cheddar cheese, grated
2 tablespoons snipped fresh chives
2 tablespoons plain flour
250ml (8fl oz/1 cup) milk

1 To make pastry, sift flour and salt into bowl. Using round-bladed knife, cut in butter until mixture resembles breadcrumbs. Gradually add water and mix to fairly stiff but pliable dough. Knead dough quickly until smooth and shape into ball. Put on to plate, cover with plastic wrap and chill for 1 hour. Roll pastry thinly into round on lightly floured work surface. Use to line tin or dish.

Trim top edges with sharp knife. Chill pastry case for 15 minutes.

2 Remove any bones from chicken. Cut flesh into bite-sized pieces.

3 Preheat oven to 230C/450F/Gas 8.

4 Gently prick pastry base with fork. Separate 1 egg. Brush a little egg white over fork holes. Beat remaining egg white with yolk and whole egg.

5 Top, tail and thinly slice courgette (zucchini). Trim spring onions (green shallots) and chop. Combine courgette and spring onions with sweetcorn in bowl. Mix in chicken and mascarpone cheese. Season with salt and pepper. Spoon into quiche. Sprinkle with cheese and chives.

6 In small bowl or jug, mix flour with a little of the milk until smooth. Stir in remaining milk and eggs. Pour over filling.

7 Bake quiche for 30 minutes until just set and golden brown. If necessary, cover pastry with foil towards end of cooking to prevent overbrowning. Turn out quiche on to plate or serve from tin or dish.

Nutritional value per portion:
4300kJ/1000 calories
Protein: 48g
Fat: 52g
Carbohydrate: 87g

Sweetcorn Quiche

Mushroom Quiche

Serves 6

Oyster mushrooms add a distinctive, subtle quiche to this quiche. If preferred, button mushrooms may be used instead.

Preparation time: about 1 hour
Baking time: about 30 minutes

FOR BAKING
25cm/10in greased flan tin or dish

SHORTCRUST PASTRY
250g (8oz/2 cups) plain flour
Pinch of salt
125g (4oz) cold butter or mixture of butter
and margarine
90ml (3fl oz/⅓ cup) cold water to mix

FILLING
500g (1lb) oyster mushrooms
3 spring onions (green shallots)
1 medium onion
2 tablespoons sunflower or corn oil
2 eggs
155g (5oz) low-fat soft cheese or fromage frais
2 tablespoons plain flour
250ml (8fl oz/1 cup) milk
Salt to taste
Freshly milled pepper
4 tablespoons snipped fresh chives

1 To make pastry, sift flour and salt into bowl. Using round-bladed knife, cut in butter until mixture resembles breadcrumbs. Gradually add water and mix to fairly stiff but pliable dough. Knead dough quickly until smooth and shape into ball. Put on to plate, cover with plastic wrap and chill for 1 hour. Roll pastry thinly into round on lightly floured work surface. Use to line tin or dish. Trim top edges with sharp knife. Chill pastry case for 15 minutes.

2 Wipe mushrooms clean with cloth or kitchen paper. Quarter if large and halve if small. Trim and chop spring onions (green shallots). Peel and chop onion.

3 Heat oil in large frying pan. Add onions and sauté gently until pale golden. Add mushrooms and cook, stirring, until most of liquid has evaporated. Cool.

4 Preheat oven to 230C/450F/Gas 8.

5 Prick pastry base with fork. Separate 1 egg. Brush a little egg white over fork holes. Fill with mushroom mixture. Top with two-thirds soft cheese or fromage frais.

6 In small bowl or jug, mix flour with a little milk until smooth. Stir in remaining milk. Beat in remaining egg white, yolk and whole egg. Add salt, pepper and half the chives. Pour carefully over mushroom filling.

7 Bake quiche for 30 minutes until just set and golden brown. If necessary, cover pastry with foil towards end of cooking to prevent overbrowning. Turn out quiche on to plate or serve from tin or dish. Dot the top with remaining soft cheese or fromage frais and sprinkle with chives.

Nutritional value per portion:
2800kJ/670kcal
Protein: 24g
Fat: 38g
Carbohydrate: 53g

Mushroom Quiche

Smoked Salmon Quiche

Serves 6

Smoked salmon flavoured with horseradish makes the perfect filling for a special occasion quiche.

Preparation time: about 50 minutes
Baking time: 20-25 minutes

FOR BAKING
6 small 10cm/4in greased flan tins

SHORTCRUST PASTRY
250g (8oz/2 cups) plain flour
Pinch of salt
125g (4oz) cold butter or mixture of butter and lard
90ml (3fl oz/$\frac{1}{3}$ cup) cold water to mix

FILLING
375g (12oz) smoked salmon
1 teaspoon creamed horseradish sauce
155g (5oz) mascarpone cheese
2 eggs
1 tablespoon plain flour
155ml (5fl oz/$\frac{2}{3}$ cup) cold milk
155ml (5fl oz/$\frac{2}{3}$ cup) single (light) cream
Salt to taste
Freshly milled pepper
3 tablespoons snipped fresh dill

1 To make pastry, sift flour and salt into bowl. Using round-bladed knife, cut in butter until mixture resembles breadcrumbs. Gradually add water and mix to fairly stiff but pliable dough. Knead dough quickly until smooth and shape into ball. Put on to plate, cover with plastic wrap and chill for 1 hour. Divide pastry into 6 equal pieces. Roll each piece thinly into a round on lightly floured work surface. Use to line tins. Trim top edges with sharp knife. Chill pastry cases for 15 minutes.

2 Preheat oven to 230C/450F/Gas 8.

3 Cut salmon into 5cm (2in) wide strips and roll up. Stir horseradish into mascarpone cheese.

4 Gently prick pastry bases with fork. Separate 1 egg. Brush a little egg white over fork holes. Cover with mascarpone mixture and salmon rolls.

5 In small bowl or jug, mix flour with a little milk until smooth. Stir in remaining milk. Beat in remaining egg white, yolk, whole egg and cream. Add salt and pepper. Finely chop two-thirds of the dill. Add to milk and egg mixture. Carefully pour into quiches over filling.

6 Bake quiches for 20-25 minutes until just set and golden brown. If necessary, cover pastry with foil towards end of cooking to prevent overbrowning. Turn out quiches on to plates or serve from tins or dishes. Sprinkle tops with remaining chopped dill.

Nutritional value per portion:
3700kJ/880kcal
Protein: 34g
Fat: 62g
Carbohydrate: 45g

Smoked Salmon Quiche

Gruyère Quiche

Serves 6

Gruyère cheese adds a Continental flavour to this quiche.

Preparation time: about 55 minutes
Baking time: about 30 minutes

FOR BAKING
25cm/10in greased flan tin or dish

SHORTCRUST PASTRY
250g (8oz/2 cups) plain flour
Pinch of salt
125g (4oz) cold butter or mixture of butter
   and lard
90ml (3fl oz/⅓ cup) cold water to mix

FILLING
220g (7oz) Gruyère cheese, grated
3 eggs
1 tablespoon plain flour
100ml (3½ fl oz) milk
155g (5oz) crème fraîche
1½ teaspoons prepared Dijon mustard
Salt to taste
Freshly milled black pepper

1 To make pastry, sift flour and salt into bowl. Using round-bladed knife, cut in butter until mixture resembles breadcrumbs. Gradually add water and mix to fairly stiff but pliable dough. Knead dough quickly until smooth and shape into ball. Put on to plate, cover with plastic wrap and chill for 1 hour. Roll out pastry fairly thinly on lightly floured work surface. Use to line prepared tin or dish. Trim top edges with sharp knife. Chill for 15 minutes.

2 Preheat oven to 230C/450F/Gas 8.

3 Gently prick pastry base with fork, then sprinkle with cheese. Beat eggs in bowl until frothy.

4 In small bowl or jug, mix flour with a little of the milk until smooth. Stir in remaining milk. Beat in eggs, crème fraîche and mustard. Season with salt and pepper. Carefully spoon egg mixture into quiche over cheese.

5 Bake quiche for 30 minutes until just set and golden brown. If necessary, cover pastry with foil towards end of cooking to prevent overbrowning. Turn out quiche on to plate or serve from tin or dish.

Nutritional value per portion:
3500kJ/830kcal
Protein: 28g
Fat: 60g

Gruyère Quiche

Chicory Quiche

Serves 6

Ginger and lemon give this quiche a piquant flavour reminiscent of the Far East.

Preparation time: about 1 hour
Baking time: about 40 minutes

FOR BAKING
25cm/10in greased fluted flan tin or dish

SHORTCRUST PASTRY
375g (12oz/3 cups) plain flour
2 pinches salt
190g (6oz) cold butter or mixture of butter and lard
125ml (4fl oz/½ cup) cold water to mix

FILLING
3 medium heads chicory
1 cooking apple
1 tablespoon lemon juice
2 spring onions (green shallots)
220g (7oz) gammon steaks, rinds removed
3 eggs
155ml (5fl oz/⅔ cup) whipping cream
1 teaspoon clear honey
½ teaspoon finely grated lemon rind
2 large pinches ground ginger
100ml (3½ oz) thick soured cream
2 tablespoons sunflower or corn oil

1 To make pastry, sift flour and salt into bowl. Using round-bladed knife, cut in butter until mixture resembles breadcrumbs. Add water and mix to fairly stiff dough. Knead, wrap and chill for 1 hour.

2 Roll out two-thirds pastry on lightly floured work surface and use to line tin or dish, trim top edges with sharp knife. Roll out remaining pastry into 30cm/12in diame-

ter round for lid, see pages 18-19. Prick with fork. Transfer to board or plate and chill with pastry case until ready to fill.

3 Preheat oven to 230C/450F/Gas 8.

4 Remove outer leaves of chicory and cut cone-shaped core out of each with tip of potato peeler. Discard. Boil chicory for 3 minutes. Drain and cool. Squeeze out water with hands. Cut into 3cm (1¼ in) thick pieces. Peel, core and thinly slice apple. Toss chicory, apple slices and lemon juice in large bowl. Trim and chop spring onions (green shallots). Chop gammon. Add to chicory.

5 Gently prick pastry base with fork. Separate 1 egg. Brush a little egg white over fork holes. Beat remaining egg white with egg yolk, whole eggs, cream, honey, lemon rind, ginger and soured cream. Stir into chicory mixture. Transfer to quiche.

6 Cover filling with pastry lid, pinching edges together. Brush pastry with oil. Mark pattern on with a knife. Bake for 40 minutes until just set and golden. If necessary, cover pastry with foil towards end of cooking to prevent overbrowning. Turn on to plate or serve from tin or dish.

Nutritional value per portion:
3800kJ/900kcal
Protein: 25g
Fat: 58g
Carbohydrate: 66g

Chicory Quiche

Prawn Quiche

Serves 6

An elegant quiche, ideal for entertaining.

Preparation time: about 45 minutes
Baking time: about 30-40 minutes

FOR BAKING
25cm/10in greased flan tin or dish

SHORTCRUST PASTRY
375g (12oz/3 cups) plain flour
Pinch of salt
190g (6oz) cold butter or mixture of butter
  and lard
125ml (4 fl oz/½ cup) cold water to mix

FILLING
60g (2oz) tomato purée (paste)
155g (5oz) low-fat soft cheese or fromage
  frais
1 tablespoon sunflower or corn oil
410g (13oz) cooked peeled prawns, thawed
  and well drained if frozen
2 eggs
1 tablespoon plain flour
3 tablespoons water
250ml (8fl oz/1 cup) single (light) cream
Salt to taste
Cayenne pepper to taste
Freshly milled pepper
1 tablespoon chopped fresh basil leaves
1 teaspoon sunflower or corn oil

1 To make pastry, sift flour and salt into bowl. Using round-bladed knife, cut in butter until mixture resembles breadcrumbs. Add water and mix to stiff dough. Knead dough quickly until smooth and shape into ball. Cover with plastic wrap and chill for 1 hour.

2 Roll out two-thirds pastry on lightly floured work surface. Use to line tin or dish. Trim pastry with sharp knife.

3 Roll remaining pastry into 30cm/12in round for lid, see pages 18-19. Transfer to plate and chill until ready to fill.

4 Preheat oven to 230C/450F/Gas 8.

5 Beat tomato purée (paste) with soft cheese or fromage frais and oil. Add prawns. Prick pastry base with fork. Separate 1 egg. Brush a little egg white over fork holes. Cover with prawns mixture.

6 Whisk remaining egg white with yolk and whole egg. Mix flour with the cold water until smooth. Add cream, eggs, salt, peppers and basil. Spoon over prawns.

7 Cover filling with pastry lid, pinching edges together. Make small hole in centre of pie. decorate with pastry shapes, cut from trimmings. Brush pastry lightly with oil. Bake for 30-40 minutes until just set and golden. If necessary, cover pastry with foil towards end of cooking to prevent over-browning. Turn out on to plate or serve from tin or dish.

Nutritional value per portion:
3900kJ/930kcal
Protein: 35g
Fat: 59g
Carbohydrate: 65g

Prawn Quiche

Step-by step

1 Sift flour and salt into bowl or on to work surface. Cut in butter or margarine using round-bladed knife.

2 Continue to cut in until butter or margarine is in tiny pieces, well coated with flour and mixture starts to loosely bind together.

3 Make well in centre. Add water. Knead ingredients together by hand to make a smooth pastry.

4 Shape dough into ball and transfer to plate. Cover with plastic wrap or foil. Chill for 1 hour to allow pastry to relax.

5 Turn out pastry on to lightly floured work surface. Roll out into round, measuring about 33cm/13in for a 25cm/10in tin.

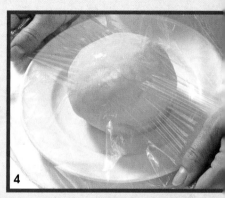

6 Brush base and sides of fluted flan tin or dish with melted butter. Line with rolled pastry, pressing it well into flutes. Take care not to stretch pastry or it will shrink during baking.

7 Trim off surplus pastry round edges with sharp kitchen knife. Cover lined tin or dish with clean tea towel. Chill for 15 minutes.

8 Prick pastry base with fork. Brush with egg white according to recipe. Add filling. Spoon or pour in egg and milk mixture.

9 Bake quiche according to recipe. To turn out, allow quiche to stand for 5 minutes. Invert quiche on to large flat plate. Lift off tin. Put serving plate on to base of quiche. Turn over so that top is facing upwards, remove first plate.